Mom, Can You Teach Me How to Invest?

A Beginner's Guide for Teens

Written by

Annette Harris

Edited by

Dweise Harris

ISBN: 979-8-9884073-3-1

To my husband, Dweise, I express my deepest gratitude for your unwavering support, love, and belief in my dreams and goals. Your constant encouragement and understanding have been the pillars of my success and happiness. Thank you for being my rock, confidant, and partner in all aspects of life.

Table of Contents

Creating A Financially Secure Future

The journey to financial independence requires consistency and commitment. It also requires a mindset of continual growth. Destiny and her older brother Trey continuously ask their mom more and more questions about money and how it all works. Throughout their journey, Destiny and Trey have learned about the basics of money, saving, and budgeting their income to achieve their future goals. Now, they want to learn what it takes to grow their income so they can have a secure financial future into adulthood.

On the journey, their mom will teach them the basics of investing and the risks and rewards of the different types of investments. There will be ups and downs as they embark on their journey, but, in the end, they will find comfort in knowing that they are growing to become financially responsible adults.

Beyond Compound Interest

"Mom, in my economics course in school, the teacher talked about investing in the stock market. She said there are different things you can invest in, like stocks, bonds, and something called ETFs. It was a lot of information, but I want to learn more about it," said Destiny.

"What more do you want to learn that she didn't cover?" asked Mom.

"Well, growing up, you taught me and Trey about compound interest. Is investing in the stock market similar to putting your money in a savings account and watching your money grow from month to month?" asked Destiny.

"Not exactly. Putting your money in a savings account has seemingly low risks because you're putting your money in a type of account with a bank where the interest is not tied to the stock market fluctuations. So, you have a very low chance of losing your money even if the bank fails because your money is protected by the FDIC up to a certain limit," said Mom.

"Okay, Mom. I have two questions. First, what is the FDIC? And, what is risk?" asked Destiny.

"Those are both great questions. The FDIC is the Federal Deposit Insurance Corporation, which applies to most banks. The FDIC protects the money you put into the bank up to $250,000. This means that if the bank fails, you can get your money back. You may not have that amount of money now, but you might in the future. So, it's important to spread your money out at different banks to protect it," said Mom.

Trey walks into the living room, exhausted and smelling of freshly cut grass after helping Dad in the yard.

"I overheard you all talking about protecting your money. My money is protected well in my bank account and under my mattress. Did something happen?" asked Trey curiously.

Destiny and Mom burst into laughter.

"No, nothing happened. I learned about investing in school today, and Mom was just about to explain the risk of investing," explained Destiny.

"Why don't you go clean up, and we can discuss the risk levels when it comes to investing?" said Mom.

"Cool! I'll be right back!" said Trey excitedly.

What is Risk?

Fresh out of the shower, Trey walked into the kitchen to join Mom and Destiny—the aroma of freshly baked cookies filled the kitchen. Trey perched on a barstool, gnawing on a cookie, while Destiny, laser-focused, leaned against the counter, notebook in hand. Mom, stirring a cup of coffee, glanced over with a smile.

"So, are you two ready to learn about risk?" she asked, her voice tinged with enthusiasm.

"Absolutely!" Destiny declared, her eyes gleaming with anticipation. "I want to fund my future business using my cash, Mom."

Trey chuckled. "Yeah, and maybe buy you a vacation home."

Mom laughed. "Ambitious, I see. But before business funding and vacation homes, you need to understand the ground rules. And that starts with risk."

She pulled up a chair and faced them. First, risks are classified into three broad levels – low-risk, medium-risk, and high-risk. Low risk is like walking in shallow water. The water's calm: maybe you get splashed when a small wave comes in, but there's little danger of getting knocked over."

Destiny scribbled furiously. "So, like putting your money in a savings account?"

"It's very similar," Mom said. "Safe, steady growth, like watching a plant sprout slowly." Trey frowned. "So, it's not different from what we've been doing with our money."

"Not necessarily," countered Mom. "Because there's still a risk of loss when you invest even in low-risk investments.

7

But it's the foundation – the secure base from which you build bigger things." She paused, then added, "And let's be honest, it's good to have some calm water when the investment waves get rough."

Destiny nodded, intrigued. "So, what's medium-risk?"

Mom's smile widened. "Picture yourself riding a surfboard. Then, you're catching some waves, feeling the thrill of the ride, but there's a chance you might wipe out. Similarly, you invest in things like stocks, maybe some real estate, which has the potential to grow quickly but may also experience some occasional dips."

Trey's eyes lit up. "Like rollercoasters? I love rollercoasters!"

"Exactly," said Mom, chuckling. "Excitement with a bit of a drop, but you know you'll eventually reach the end, safe and sound."

Destiny frowned. "But what about high-risk? Is that like jumping off a diving board?"

"Well, not quite," said Mom, with a hint of caution. "Think of it like deep-sea diving. You're exploring the unknown, potentially finding amazing treasures, but there's a real danger if you don't know what you're doing. These are things like starting your own business, moving out on your own, where the rewards can be huge, but the risks are also high."

Trey whistled. "Sounds intense."

"It is," Mom agreed. "And that's why most people start low, build their skills and knowledge, then gradually venture into deeper waters. Remember that every risk comes with a potential reward, but there are also possible downsides."

Destiny twirled the pen in her hand. "So, Mom, where would you say we are now?"

Mom grinned. "Right now, you're still dipping your toes in the shallows, building your sandcastle. But with a little time, learning, and experience, you'll be riding waves and maybe even deep-sea diving for treasure. Just remember, you must determine what level of risk you are comfortable with when investing."

"Thanks, mom. So, what are the different types of investment options that we can explore?" asked Trey curiously.

"We can definitely talk about your options, but who wants another cookie first?" Mom said, smiling.

"Me!" said Destiny and Trey in unison.

Low-Risk Options

"Are you ready to learn about some amazing low-risk options that can help you grow your wealth? As beginners in the world of finance, let's start with high-yield savings accounts, savings bonds, and certificates of deposit or CDs. With these accounts, you can earn compound interest and watch your money grow at a much faster rate than a regular savings account. Get ready to embark on an exciting journey towards financial prosperity! Let's begin," exclaimed Mom with enthusiasm.

High-Yield Savings Accounts

Trey crunched another cookie, a thoughtful munch. "But Mom, low-risk sounds...slow. Wouldn't we miss out on all the fast stuff?"

Destiny nodded, her pen poised over her notebook. "Yeah, like, why not just jump straight into those deep-sea investments? Get rich quick, you know?"

Mom chuckled, shaking her head. "Tempting, I know. But remember that roller coaster analogy? You wouldn't climb on without a harness, right? Low-risk options are your harness, your seatbelt in the financial world. They protect you while you continue to learn."

Destiny nodded, understanding the analogy. "So, it's important to start with low-risk options, get comfortable with potential gains and losses, and increase my wealth over time."

"That's right," said Mom as she grabbed a glass, pouring each of them a cup of milk.

"Now, high-yield savings accounts are like those kiddie pools in the water park. Sure, they won't give you the adrenaline rush of the big slides, but you're guaranteed to have fun and stay safe. Your money grows steadily, protected by the FDIC we discussed earlier."

Trey raised an eyebrow. "FDIC? Sounds like a superhero."

"That's right, you missed that part, but you're not that far off," Mom winked. "As I mentioned to Destiny earlier, the FDIC promises to keep your money safe up to a certain amount, even if the bank gets splashed by a financial wave."

Destiny tapped her pen. "So, it's like a guaranteed return, even if it's small?"

"Exactly!" Mom smiled. "And here's the magic – that small, steady growth multiplies over time. It's called compound interest, like earning interest on your interest. It's like planting an orange tree, watching it grow and flower, then letting it bear fruit year after year. The longer you keep your money in, the bigger and sweeter the harvest."

"I remember now, Mom, we talked about compound interest when I was learning about saving, and you said it was like our orange trees in the backyard. It's all coming back to me now!" said Destiny excitedly.

Trey considered this, squinting at his empty cookie plate. "It's also like making cookies, right?" he thought. "The more dough you mix, the more cookies you get. Similarly, the more money you save, the more you earn in interest."

"Precisely!" Mom exclaimed, patting his hand. "And just like you wouldn't throw all your ingredients in at once, hoping for a giant cake, you wouldn't invest everything in high-risk options. Low-yield accounts are your basic flour and sugar,

11

the foundation for your financial baking. They keep your money safe while it slowly rises, ready for when you're ready to add the colorful toppings and the fancy icing of riskier investments."

Destiny's eyes widened. "So, even though it's slow, does saving money in a high-yield savings account help build something?" she asked her mom.

"Absolutely," Mom replied. "Every penny you save is a brick used to build your financial house. As you continue to build, you'll eventually have a skyscraper. And who knows, maybe you'll have enough leftover bricks to build that vacation home for me one day."

They all shared a laugh.

I Bonds

Destiny's scribbles filled page after page while Trey munched on a stray cookie crumb, his mind buzzing with possibilities.

"Okay, Mom," said Destiny, her eyes gleaming with entrepreneurial spirit. "High-yield accounts are like the safe starting point, but what about building that empire? What's the next step?"

Mom's smile widened. "Glad you asked, *CEO* Destiny. Let's talk about savings bonds. There are two types of bonds: I Bonds and EE Bonds. I've been buying bonds, I Bonds, and EE bonds since you and Trey were babies. I'll explain I Bonds first, said Mom.

I Bonds are a type of savings bond sold by the government. I want you to think of I Bonds as buried treasure chests that grow with the tide of inflation. I Bonds earn interest based on two things: a fixed rate and the rate of inflation. The **fixed rate** is a sturdy chain that stays the same and never changes, so you receive a guaranteed minimum interest rate when you buy the bond. The **inflation rate,** on the other hand, ebbs and flows like the tide. When inflation is high, the chains pull hard, lifting your chest (your investment) higher. When inflation is low, the chains loosen up but keeps your chest above the waves.

"That sounds interesting, so how do they work together," Destiny asked.

"Together, the fixed and inflation-adjusted rates keep your buried treasure (your I-bond investment) safe from the rising tide of inflation. Even if the waves grow, your treasure stays protected and rises with the tide, so your money doesn't get eaten away by inflation," explained Mom.

Trey's eyebrows shot up. "Treasure chests? Cool!"

Destiny tapped her pen. "But isn't that just like a regular savings account?"

"Nope," Mom said, shaking her head. "Regular accounts just sit there, watching the inflation waves roll by. I Bonds, on the other hand, fight back. They earn a fixed interest rate, like a hidden bonus, on top of the inflation bump."

Trey's eyes narrowed. "Hidden bonus? That sounds awesome. So, we bury our money, and it just grows?" Trey asked.

"Not quite," Mom cautioned. "There are some rules. You can't cash them out for at least a year, and if you do before five years, you lose part of that hidden bonus. Think of it like a small fee for early access. Let me show you a chart I created to monitor potential interest penalties when withdrawing my I-bonds early." Mom said.

I BOND EARLY WITHDRAWAL PENALTY

WITHIN THE FIRST YEAR
You lose all the bonus gold coins! Your treasure chest only grows by the fixed interest rate, like a regular savings account.

BETWEEN 1 AND 5 YEARS
You lose some of the bonus coins, depending on how early you withdraw. The longer you hold the I Bond, the fewer coins the thief takes, and the more your treasure grows with inflation.

AFTER 5 YEARS
You keep all the bonus gold coins! Your treasure chest gets the full benefit of both the fixed and inflation-adjusted rates.

Destiny frowned. "Five years? That's ages! But is it worth it in the long run?"

"Absolutely!" Mom said. "Let's say you put $1000 in an I-bond today. Over 20 years, with an excellent interest rate, it could grow to almost $2800! Remember, it's a long-term investment. Like planting an orange tree – you nurture it for years, but eventually, you get delicious orange juice, right?"

Trey grinned. "Fresh squeezed orange juice is worth waiting for."

Destiny nodded, her pen tapping thoughtfully. "So, I-bonds are good for long-term goals, like my business?"

"Absolutely," Mom said. "They're a safe way to build your financial fortress, brick by inflation-protected brick."

Trey piped up, eyes dreamy. "And what about me, Mom? I want to save for that vacation home for you. Can I use I Bonds for that?"

Mom's heart warmed. "Of course, honey. It's a perfect way to show love and build your nest egg. Just remember, every penny saved is a step closer to that real estate empire that you've been dreaming of."

EE Bonds

"Mom," began Destiny, "you mentioned EE bonds. What are those, and how are they different from I Bonds?"

"Here's where EE bonds come in. EE bonds are like slow-cooker investments. You put your money in at a low temperature and let it simmer for a long time – 20 years, to be exact. But here's the payoff: when you finally cash in that bond, your $50 could be worth $100 or even more! That's like finding $20 in an old pair of jeans hidden in your closet," said Mom.

Destiny scribbled furiously. "So, what about inflation? If prices go up, does the value of my EE Bond go up?"

"Not quite," said Mom. "Think of it like a guaranteed growth rate instead of inflation protection. EE Bonds come with a fixed interest rate set when you buy them. It's like knowing the exact speed that your money grows – slow and steady, but reliable."

"So, it's like a predictable journey, unlike the ups and downs of the I Bond waves?" asked Trey.

"Exactly," Mom confirmed. "And the best part is they're guaranteed to double in value after 20 years."

"Whoa, that is like finding a hidden $20 in my jeans pocket! I think that's a better option than I Bonds," Trey exclaimed.

"It can be," Mom agreed. "But remember, unlike I Bonds, EE Bonds don't adjust for inflation."

Destiny frowned. "So, I-bonds are better for uncertain times, while EE Bonds are more predictable but might not keep up with inflation?"

"Yes," said Mom.

Trey scratched his chin, pondering this. "So, it's all about what kind of adventure we want, right?"

"Precisely," Mom beamed. "Both I Bonds and EE Bonds offer safe investments for your money but take different routes. Deciding which one is closer to your dreams is up to you."

"Do EE Bonds have penalties for withdrawing them early, too?" asked Trey.

"Yes, the interest penalty on EE Bonds is similar to I Bonds for the first five years. After five years, you won't lose the interest you earned. However, if you cash in your EE Bonds before 20 years, you will be subject to an early withdrawal penalty. If you cash in your bonds after 20 years, there will be no early withdrawal penalty, but you will miss out on the interest you could earn until the maturity date, which is 30 years from the purchase date. Therefore, before buying an EE Bond, it's best to determine if you're willing to keep it for the long haul so that you don't miss out on any potential interest earnings," explained Mom.

Certificates of Deposit

As Mom finished explaining bonds, Trey, who had been fidgeting during the longer conversation, suddenly froze. He glanced at Destiny, eyes wide, then scrambled for his backpack. "Whoa, wait, I gotta write all this down!" he exclaimed, brandishing his notebook and pen like a newly discovered treasure.

"Alright, are you ready to dive a little deeper?" Mom asked.

Destiny and Trey nodded.

"Let's talk about Certificates of Deposit or CDs. CDs are an investment that can offer you peace of mind like no other. CDs offer predictable and guaranteed returns with little to no risk. This makes them perfect for people who don't want to worry about market fluctuations or other uncertainties. With CDs, you can sit back, relax, and watch your money grow – all while knowing that the FDIC protects your investment.

Trey scribbled in his notebook. "Guaranteed returns? Sounds amazing! Like never-ending interest?"

"Not quite, Trey. CDs offer fixed interest rates for a set period, like six months, a year, or even several years. It's like locking in a special price for a new video game – you know exactly what you'll get and pay when it's released."

Trey's eyebrows shot up. "But what if I change my mind? Can't I just cancel the order?"

"Sure, you can cash out early," explained Mom. "But it's like leaving the buffet before eating dessert – you might have to pay an early withdrawal penalty. It's a fee for changing your mind. Basically, you're allowing the bank to hold your money, and they lend it to others or use it for other investment opportunities. If you take your money out of the CD early, the bank has to find another way to fund its business."

Destiny frowned. "So, the bank would use my money and give it to others?"

"Yes, but remember your money is protected, and you can check your account to see that the funds from your CD are in your account and earning interest," explained Mom.

Destiny smiled. "Okay. So, it's a commitment, but worth it for more money in the end?"

"Exactly!" Mom said. "And the longer you commit, the sweeter the reward. The interest you earn will vary based on how long you commit to the CD and the bank's current interest rate offers. It can vary daily. So, I suggest looking for CDs with fixed rates, and when you see a CD with a high interest rate, you should strongly consider it as an investment option."

Trey pondered this. "Wait. So, at the end of the CD, what happens? Do we get a giant treasure chest of interest?"

"You have options. You can cash out your CD and put the money back into your savings account, or you can put it into another type of investment. You can renew the CD with the updated interest rate. Renewing the CD allows you to reinvest your money and the interest you earned," explained Mom.

Destiny's eyes sparkled. "Reinvest it? Like compounding?"

"Exactly!" exclaimed Mom. "Let's say you invest $5,000 in a one-year CD earning 4% interest. You'll have earned $200 in the end. Now, if you reinvest that interest, it joins the principal for next year's ride, earning you even more."

Trey whistled. "Sounds like a snowball rolling down a mountain of money!"

"The power of compound interest," said Mom.

Destiny and Trey exchanged excited glances. CDs no longer seemed boring; they were keys to unlocking their financial goals, a steady drive towards freedom.

"All right, kids, you've learned a lot for now. Let's take a break while you consider what we've discussed. Help me clean up in the kitchen, and we can discuss moderate-risk investment options next weekend," said Mom.

Destiny and Trey looked at each other, their eyes wide with anticipation.

Reflection Questions

When investing, it's important to consider your short-term and long-term goals. Use the questions below to help you determine what you want to achieve throughout your investment journey.

1. What are your investment goals? What do you want to save for?

2. Why are you interested in investing? Is it to grow your wealth, to learn about the market, or for something else?

3. What types of low-risk investments have you learned about?

4. What resources will you use to learn more about investing?

Moderate-Risk Options

The following weekend, Mom, Trey, and Destiny ate lunch at their favorite restaurant. As Destiny stirred her French onion soup, the onions swirled like a question mark. She couldn't help but bring up the topic of investing again. "So, Mom, you said medium-risk investments are like... stepping stones to higher returns, right?"

Their mom smiled; her salad gleamed with crisp romaine and ruby-red pomegranate seeds. "Exactly! They offer a bit more potential for growth than low-risk options but with a little more wiggle room in terms of price fluctuations."

Trey, ever the pragmatist, speared a chunk of grilled chicken.

"Wiggle room? Like, a rollercoaster that dips a bit but doesn't throw you off the tracks?"

Mom chuckled. "That's a good analogy! Think of it like hiking a scenic trail. Low-risk investments are like paved paths, smooth and predictable. Medium-risk investments are like well-maintained dirt trails, maybe a bit steeper, with some rocks to navigate, but the views are more rewarding."

Destiny's eyes lit up. "So, what kind of investments are included in medium-risk investments?" asked Destiny.

"There's a whole range of options!" Mom gestured with her fork. "Like mutual funds and exchange-traded funds or Exchange-Traded Funds. Let's discuss mutual funds first."

Mutual Funds

"Imagine you and Trey want to climb a mountain to see the best view, but you both have different levels of experience. You, Destiny, prefer a gentle, winding path with pretty flowers and lookout points. Trey, since you're always looking for adventure, you may want a steeper trail with exciting challenges and hidden waterfalls," said Mom.

"A mutual fund is like a group adventure to the top, where everyone pools their money to hire a professional guide – also known as the fund manager," continued Mom. "It's sort of like the tour guides we use when we go on vacation. This guide knows the mountain well and picks different paths for everyone based on their comfort level," said Mom.

"So, it's like when I want to go on an eating tour, and Trey wants to go snorkeling. I want something easy and not too stressful, and Trey is looking for adventure and excitement; our preferences differ," commented Destiny.

"Yes," said Mom. "Destiny, for you, the guide might choose a low-risk trail, like a wide, paved path. It's not as exciting, but it's safe and steady. You won't climb super high, but you'll enjoy the scenery and have a peaceful journey."

"Okay, I get it now," said Trey. "So, while I go snorkeling, Destiny's going to stay on the boat and feed the fish. She's going to have fun, but her feet will be on steady ground."

"Absolutely!" said Mom excitedly. Trey, the guide might choose a medium-risk trail for your mutual fund, like a well-maintained dirt path with some steeper climbs and maybe a few rocks to navigate. It's a bit more challenging, but the views are amazing, like investing in stocks of growing companies or smaller, less established ones. You might climb higher and faster, but there could be some bumps as the companies grow."

"That sounds intriguing, scary, and fun all at the same time," said Destiny.

"It can be," said Mom. "The fun part is that there are tons of different trails! Just like there are many types of mutual funds, each with its own focus and level of risk. Remember, the key is to tell the guide what you're comfortable with and what you want to see. They can then choose the best trail for you and Trey."

Exchange-Traded Funds (ETFs)

Destiny scraped the last bit of cheese from her French onion soup, a satisfied sigh escaping her lips. "Mom," she asked, "You mentioned another medium-risk investment, right? What about those... exchange-traded funds, or ETFs? How do those work?"

Trey, ever the picture of teenage skepticism, crossed his arms. "Yeah, ETFs. Sounds like something you'd find in a dusty library, not an exciting investment."

Mom chuckled, her eyes twinkling. "Not at all, Trey! Think of ETFs like those grab-and-go salad bars at the grocery store."

Destiny's eyes widened. "The ones with all the different toppings?"

"Exactly! ETFs are like pre-made baskets of investments, already filled with stocks, bonds, and even commodities like gold or oil. You choose the one that suits your taste, buy shares, and there you have it: instant diversification!"

Trey raised an eyebrow. "But why not just pick the stocks yourself, like customizing your salad?"

"That's like trying to juggle a dozen different vegetables while walking a tightrope," explained Mom. "It's a lot of work, and if you drop one, it can be messy. ETFs do the juggling for you, mixing and matching the right ingredients based on a specific theme or strategy."

"Like a chef's salad or a spring mix with a bit of everything?" Destiny guessed.

"Exactly! Some ETFs track broad market indexes, like a classic Caesar with romaine and parmesan, giving you exposure to a variety of companies. Others focus on specific sectors, like a spicy Thai salad with chili peppers and lemongrass, offering higher potential returns but also a bit more heat."

"So, it's like having a whole buffet of *investment salads* to choose from?" Trey mused, his skepticism slowly melting.

"Precisely! And just like you wouldn't load up your salad with every topping available, you must also be careful while investing in ETFs. Take your time to research them carefully and choose the ones that match your risk tolerance and goals. And always remember, diversification is key. So, don't just invest in the hottest or newest ETF, or you may end up getting burnt." said Mom.

"That's a very clever way to put it, Mom," said Trey.

"Thank you, Trey," said Mom, smiling as she took the final bite of her salad. "Now that we're all finished with our meal, let's head home."

Destiny and Trey shared a smile. The world of ETFs, once a confusing combination of letters, was finally making sense. They could almost visualize themselves selecting from a virtual salad bar of investments.

As they left the soup and salad bar with full stomachs and buzzing minds from the newfound knowledge, they eagerly anticipated learning about high-risk investments from their mom.

Reflection Questions

Navigating moderate-risk investments means navigating potential ups and downs for higher returns. Use the questions below to ponder your comfort level with the risks and rewards.

1. What types of moderate-risk investments are you interested in?

2. What level of risk are you comfortable with? Are you willing to accept possible losses of your investment for the chance of greater gains? Why?

3. How will you track and monitor your portfolio performance?

4. How can you seek valuable insights and perspectives by discussing your investment decisions with family or mentors?

High-Risk Options

Later that evening, after they arrived home, Destiny and Trey were seated beside Mom in the home office, surrounded by crumpled worksheets and discarded markers. The sunset streamed through the window, dappling their faces with a warm glow.

"Let me tell you how I started investing for you, Trey and Destiny," Mom began. "While I had set up savings accounts for you both, I also wanted to provide a higher return on the money you'll receive when you're older and more responsible. So, I opened a custodial account for each of you, which allows me to invest in various stocks, ETFs, corporate bonds, and other investment options available in the stock market.

I have been extremely careful in picking the investments for your accounts. I thoroughly researched every fund or stock before investing in it. Now, when you become legally mature and knowledgeable about making high-risk investment decisions, the account will be solely your responsibility," explained Mom.

"So, Mom," began Destiny, tilting her chin up, "how do we get a taste of high-risk investing if you're in control of the custodial account?" asked Destiny.

"Good question!" said Mom, smiling, pulling up a colorful pie chart on her computer screen. "Think of this account as your very own investment playground. It's where I can help you experiment and learn with a little real-world investing practice, with safeguards, of course."

Trey, who always saw things realistically, said, "So, like the training wheels that used to be on our bikes?"

"Exactly!" said Mom, laughing. "The concept is the same because the training wheels come off eventually. Again, when you become legally mature, generally between the ages of 18 to 21, this account becomes all yours, and you'll be responsible for managing and balancing it."

"Sounds scary, but I think we can handle it with more practice and research," said Trey.

"I agree," said Mom. "Now, let's talk about individual stocks and fractional shares and how they can be purchased through your custodial account."

Individual Stocks

Trey and Destiny's eyes were glued to the computer screen. Their custodial account was a new journey in their financial education. Both of their accounts held a modest sum, but they were ready to dive into the world of individual stocks.

"So," said Mom, "are you two excited about picking your own stocks?"

"Yes!" Trey exclaimed, his enthusiasm bubbling over. "I'm thinking about that technology company that makes new and innovative car products everyone's talking about."

Destiny, ever the cautious one, furrowed her brow. "But Mom, you said individual stocks are risky, right?"

Mom nodded. "They are. Unlike mutual funds, which spread your money across many companies, individual stocks are for one specific business. If the company you invest in does well, you can earn a lot of money. But if the company struggles, you could lose most or all the money you invested."

Trey frowned. "So, we shouldn't buy cool stocks like the technology company?" Trey asked inquisitively.

"Not necessarily," said Mom. "You can invest in some of the "cooler" companies, but you have to do your research to evaluate the history of the stock. Together, we'll research how the company has performed over the last one, five, or even ten years to determine if it's a smart investment. We'll learn about their financials and make sure we understand the risks before we put any money in. That's the beauty of a custodial account."

Destiny's eyes lit up. "So, it's like a team effort?"

"Exactly!" Mom agreed. "We'll learn together, make informed decisions, and hopefully, build a strong portfolio over time. Remember, it's not just about making money quickly. It's about understanding the market, taking calculated risks, and learning from both successes and failures."

Trey grinned. "Okay, team! Let's do this. But first, can we research that technology company? I'm still curious about it."

Mom smiled. "Of course. But remember, just because you are interested in the technology they create for cars doesn't necessarily mean that investing in the company will be a good idea. You still need to do your homework and research the company thoroughly."

Mom, Trey, and Destiny spent the afternoon digging into the world of individual stocks. They learned about balance sheets, income statements, and market trends. They discussed the potential risks and rewards of investing in different companies.

Trey and Destiny found that companies they initially thought would be good investments. However, after doing their research, they concluded that they were not the best for them financially when they evaluated the company's historical performance. As they continued their research, they came across the term "dividends," leading Trey to ask his mom about them. "What are the dividends that some of these stocks have?" he asked.

"That's an excellent question, Trey," said his mom enthusiastically. "Let me explain what dividends are and why some companies pay them while others don't."

Dividends

"Let's imagine you own a lemonade stand," Mom said.

"Every time you sell lemonade, you might make a little profit. I want you to imagine that your lemonade stand was so successful that you could afford to share some of that profit with your best friends, maybe give them a free cup of lemonade every week. That's kind of like a dividend!"

"When investing in stocks, a dividend is a share of the company's profits that gets paid out to its shareholders, like you and me," continued Mom. "A shareholder is someone who owns one or more stock of a company. Now, imagine you own shares in a company that makes bicycles. If they have a great year and sell lots of bicycles, they might share some of that success with their shareholders by paying a dividend. That means each shareholder would get a small payment for each share they own, like a mini-reward for being part of the team!"

Trey piped in and said, "So, it's just like sharing the lemonade with our friends. They bought lemonade from us, we made a profit, and we're offering them the free lemonade."

"You're absolutely correct!" said mom excitedly. "But here's the catch, not all companies are lemonade stands with overflowing cups of profit. Some companies, like startups, might reinvest all their earnings or profit into growing the business. This means they might not have any extra cash to share with shareholders, so they don't pay dividends."

"So, what are they doing with all the money they made as a profit?" asked Destiny curiously.

"They're using all their lemonade money, or profits, to buy bigger lemons and fancier cups!" explained Mom. "When companies do this, they're trying to attract more business so they can continue to grow. For example, they might want to use it to hire more employees, buy new equipment, create new products, or even buy back their own shares to make them more valuable."

"So, it's like they're using their lemonade money to build a bigger stand, open another location, or even upgrade their recipe!" said Trey.

"You're catching on," said Mom.

"So, why would anyone want to invest in a company that doesn't pay dividends?" asked Destiny.

"Well, it's all about hope! These companies might be growing really fast, and their stock price could grow in the future. You take your chances by betting that the company will be one of the best in its industry, even if you're not getting dividends yet," explained Mom.

"Remember, like with any investment, there's always risk involved. Some companies that don't pay dividends might never take off, and their stock price could even fall. So, it's important to research and understand why a company doesn't pay dividends before investing in it."

Trey and Destiny pondered this information while they continued to research companies to invest in. Trey found many exciting companies, but some of the stocks cost more than he budgeted for investing.

"Mom, these stocks are really expensive. How can I afford any of them?" asked Trey.

"Both of you have been asking some excellent questions, and that's another crucial one," said Mom, smiling. "There is a different way for you to buy stocks, called fractional shares. By using this method, you can afford stocks that would otherwise be outside of your budget. Let's take a fifteen-minute break to stretch our legs, and we can go over fractional shares in more detail when we return."

Fractional Shares

"Okay, team," Mom announced after a refreshing ice-water break, "let's dive into the final high-risk frontier: fractional shares." Trey and Destiny, still buzzing from dividends, leaned closer, eyes wide with anticipation.

"Imagine you see the coolest sneakers ever," began Mom, "but they cost $300! That's a lot for a pair of shoes, right?" asked Mom.

Trey chuckled. "Maybe for you, Mom, but we understand where you're going with this analogy."

"Okay!" chuckled Mom. "Well, let's say they're $500, and you can't afford to purchase the newest sneakers as a pair. Meaning you could only buy either the left shoe or the right shoe in one purchase. But what if you could still own the left shoe now and maybe buy the right shoe later?" asked Mom.

"I don't know if I only want to own one shoe," said Trey as he pondered, imagining himself walking around with one new shoe and an old shoe.

"Well, it's your gateway to buying what you really want, only you buy it a little at a time. That's where fractional shares come in," said Mom.

"Well, it's your gateway to buying what you really want, only you buy it a little at a time. That's where fractional shares come in. You know, get one foot in the door," said Mom with a grin.

Trey and Destiny found Mom's pun funny and started giggling. "Mom, that was very clever," Trey said.

"Thank you, Trey," replied Mom.

Destiny appeared intrigued and asked, "So, fractional shares? Does that mean you buy a small piece of a share?"

"Exactly!" exclaimed Mom. "It's like buying a slice of cheesecake instead of the whole cheesecake. You still get to taste the deliciousness, but you only pay for what you can eat and afford today."

"Let me break it down further," said Mom. "Suppose there is a stock that costs $200, but you only have $20 to invest. Instead of waiting until you have $200, you can purchase a fractional share of the stock using your $20. This way, you won't have to wait to invest in the company, and you can still receive any dividends or returns on the stock while you're waiting to invest more," explained Mom.

Trey raised his eyebrows. "So, we could buy a fraction of a share or stock even though it costs a hundred slices of cheesecake?"

"Absolutely!" confirmed Mom. "You could own a tiny piece of a company you believe in, even if the full share price is out of reach. It's a great way to diversify your portfolio and get exposure to exciting companies without going over your budget."

Destiny thought for a minute. "But Mom, what if the company flops, and our little slice of cheesecake crumbles? Isn't that risky?" asked Destiny.

Mom nodded. "Risk is always there. That's why you shouldn't put all your eggs in one fractional basket."

She pulled up a chart on the screen, highlighting a few companies with fractional share options. "See these? They're all innovative, fast-growing companies, but their full share prices are pretty high. By buying a fraction, you're betting on their future potential, but you're also spreading out the risk."

Destiny pondered this. "So, it's about taking calculated risks and believing that we are making the best decision for long-term success?"

Trey added, "And it's like we're committing our resources, our money, with hopes of achieving benefits later."

"Exactly!" exclaimed Mom, beaming with pride. "Fractional shares can be a powerful investment tool, but they come with a high level of risk and require careful research and understanding. It is important to remember, just like with anything else, that you should never spend or invest more than you can afford to lose. And, before making any investment decisions, always do your homework and diversify your portfolio to protect yourself from financial ruin."

"One second, Mom," said Destiny. "You've mentioned diversification a couple of times. What exactly does that mean?"

"Well, since we've covered low, moderate, and high-level risk investment options, let's talk a little bit more about diversifying your investments across each risk level," said Mom.

Reflection Questions

Investing in high-risk options can result in major financial losses, which could negatively affect your long-term financial objectives. Therefore, it's crucial to grasp the fundamental financial concepts, cultivate good saving habits, and explore safer investment avenues first. Once you have a good understanding of financial literacy, have a conversation with an adult before considering high-risk investment options.

Here are some questions to ponder, solely for educational purposes:

1. What are the emotional risks associated with high-risk investing?

2. How volatile are high-risk investments?

3. Are your financial goals best served by high-risk investments?

4. What are some alternative ways to invest my time and resources that could benefit my future?

Diversifying Your Portfolio

Investing your money wisely is crucial for securing your financial future. Diversifying your portfolio is one of the most effective ways to ensure that your investments remain profitable and secure. Diversifying your investments means spreading your money across different types of assets so that your portfolio is not overly reliant on one type of investment. This approach can help you minimize risk and increase your chances of achieving your financial goals. With this context in mind, we'll review how diversifying your investment portfolio is similar to trying different subjects in school until you find the ones that help you chart your path in life.

"Okay, let's talk about diversifying your investment portfolio," Mom said. Diversifying your investments is like changing majors in college until you find the one that is more interesting or has more career options for your path in life. If you're not engaged or motivated while pursuing your current major, you may want to switch to another one that aligns with your goals the following year. This is similar to diversifying your investment portfolio because you get to see what works for you and spread out the risk of potentially not passing a course with an A and staying on the dean's list."

"Diversification is having a list full of investments to choose from. You spread your money across different types of low, moderate, and high-risk investments and choose the different options to explore."

Destiny chimed in. "But why wouldn't we just stick to the safest option, the low-risk choices?"

"Remember," Mom explained, "sometimes the safest option might not lead you to achieving your goals with the timeline you have established. And even if you choose the safest path, you may still encounter unexpected challenges. Consider this analogy: if you put all your eggs in one basket, and that basket falls, you run the risk of losing your eggs. But if you spread your eggs across several baskets, even if one basket falls, you still have eggs in the other baskets. So, the best way to minimize risks and maximize gains is to invest in a mix of all three risk levels based on your personal goals and risk tolerance."

"I get it," said Trey. "We shouldn't invest all of our money in stocks with just one company because if something happens and that company fails, we could lose most or all of our money. But, if we also invested in CDs, ETFs, or Mutual Funds, we would still have other investments to fall back on.

"Yes," confirmed Mom. "Even if you're comfortable with taking risks, it's important to have some low-risk investments to ensure financial security. This applies to all investors, including the most risk-tolerate ones."

"It's like packing for a long journey," continued Mom. "You wouldn't bring only one type of clothing for every possible weather condition. You'd pack a variety of clothes to be prepared for different situations. The same is true for investing. By diversifying your portfolio, you're preparing yourself for different market conditions and reducing your overall risk."

Trey and Destiny nodded, understanding showing on their faces. They were eager to start building their own diversified portfolios, ready to navigate the investing world with a balanced approach.

As the sun dipped below the horizon, casting long shadows in the office, Mom looked at her children with pride.

"Remember," she said, her voice soft, "the best investment you can make is in yourselves. Keep learning, keep exploring, and never be afraid to ask questions. Together, we'll build a portfolio that can weather any financial storm."

Trey and Destiny exchanged grins, their eyes brimming with the promise of a future filled with adventure, knowledge, and a bright financial horizon. The adventure had just begun.

Definitions

Commodity – A physical product that can be bought, sold, or exchanged for a similarly priced product. Examples include wheat, an essential ingredient in bread, pasta, and other food items. Metals like iron, aluminum, copper, gold, and silver are commodities used in jewelry and constructing bridges and buildings.

Compound Interest – Money earned on your initial investment that accumulates interest from the previous investment period.

Diversification – Spreading the money you invest across different types of low, moderate, and high-risk investment options.

Fluctuation – The constant up and down of prices of stocks and bonds in the stock market.

Investment – Putting your money into something like a company that grows in value over time to sell it in the future for a profit.

Shareholder – Someone who owns a stock or share of a company and is eligible for a share of the company's profits.

Acknowledgments

I want to acknowledge and express my gratitude to my amazing husband, Dweise, who worked tirelessly to edit multiple versions of this book. To my wonderful children, D'Shauna, Tristan, Deja, Dontavious, and Destiny - you are a continual inspiration to me.

I would also like to extend my thanks to Sam Peak II for his valuable insights, wisdom, enthusiasm, and suggestions.

About the Author

Annette Harris is a wife, mother, and avid volunteer in her community. She is a military veteran who spent eight years in the United States Army with two wartime deployments in Afghanistan and Iraq. She graduated from Florida State University with a Juris Master's degree and Webster University and Liberty University with Master's degrees.

She now works as a human resources professional and adjunct instructor in human resources and is the owner and founder of Harris Financial Coaching.

She lives in Florida with her husband as an empty nester.

Visit her website at www.HarrisWealthCoach.com.